Let's go to Bethlehem
Edward Bennett

A PLAY FOR

The play was produced at Christchu~~~~ ~~~~st-Methodist Church, Leicester on 20th . ~~an the following cast in order of appearance:

NARRATOR   Janet Asher

JOSH   Jim Bennett

AMOS   David Eyre

SAM   Barry Weedon

BENNY   Richard Carroll

NARRATOR   I'm going to read you a story.   It's an old one, and you've heard it many times before, probably know most of it off by heart.   Still, it's the season of goodwill, and so I hope you'll be patient with me.   Well, here goes!

The Narrator reads Luke chapter 2 from verse 8, preferably from the Good News Bible.   After the opening words of verse 16 , he stops abruptly.

Have you ever wondered what they were like, those shepherds? Long gowns made of curtain material, a striped towel tied round the head and holding a shepherd's crook, merging anonymously into the decor of the nativity scene.   Our eyes and our thoughts focus naturally on the child, Jesus, lying in the manger, Mary and Joseph looking lovingly at him.   But spare a thought for those men, leaving their flocks of sheep to go down into Bethlehem in the   middle of the night to look for a baby.   They're just ordinary people, like us, who were chosen to carry the good news ... chosen - as we are chosen - and being just as inadequate as we are - to spread abroad this astonishing good news.   Makes you think, doesn't it?

Three shepherds, Sam and Amos led by Josh approach

SAM   Who said, "Let's go to Bethlehem" ?

AMOS   Josh, he said it, didn't you, Josh?

JOSH   The angel said, "In the City of David", that's Bethlehem.

SAM   Of course it's Bethlehem, but who's idea was it we should go traipsing off in the middle of the night? Who said come on, let's up and go to Bethlehem?

JOSH   All right, all right, so it was me. But we all agreed.

AMOS   The angel did seem to - well - urge us on, I suppose.

JOSH   Of course he did, and if we don't hurry it'll be daybreak before we get there.

SAM   How many miles to Bethlehem?

JOSH   Never mind how many, let's just keep going.

SAM   And what for, that's what I want to know, Josh, what for?

AMOS   To find this baby, of course.

SAM   But why us, that's what I mean. Why us? Quietly going about our lawful business on the hillside, and then there's this great voice, and lights and all that singing fit to wake the dead! Why couldn't they go straight to Bethlehem, eh, Amos, why couldn't they do that?

AMOS   I don't know, Sam. I expect they had their reasons. Maybe because it was nearer.

SAM   Nearer!

AMOS   To heaven - up on the hillside.

SAM   Wouldn't make any difference to angels. Distance is no object to them.

JOSH   Well it is to us, Sam, so let's get a move on.

Edward Bennett

LET'S GO TO BETHLEHEM

NIMBUS.
PRESS

COPYRIGHT

We are mainly interested in providing resources for churches that want to use drama in worship, in bible study and in evangelism. You do not need a license to perform any of our plays but we would be grateful if you would write and tell us about any productions you put on. All our plays are protected by copyright and so we ask that you buy copies for each actor when you purchase one. We hope that you will find them useful for the work of the Kingdom.

Fees for performances by professional companies will be subject to negotiation.

This edition 1998 Nimbus Press,
18 Guilford Road, Leicester, LE2 2RB

First published in1996

British Library Cataloguing in Publication
Data available
ISBN 1 874424 07 1

Printed in Great Britain by
Moorleys Print & Publishing, Ilkeston, Derbys.

AMOS   Could be they didn't want to wake up the whole town.

SAM   I was just enjoying a nice kip when that racket started.   Anyway, how are we going to find this baby when we get there?

JOSH   In a manger, the angel said.

SAM   Yeah, that's good, isn't it?   In a manger.   And how many mangers are there in Bethlehem?

AMOS   It's not that big a place.   We'll find it.

JOSH   It's simple.   We try the inn first.   If it's not there, they'll probably know where it is.

SAM   And if I know the innkeeper, he's not going to be best pleased being woken up at three o'clock in the morning.

JOSH   Just stop arguing, Sam, and let's go.

AMOS   Here, hang on chaps, hang on a minute.

JOSH   What's up now?

AMOS   Benny isn't with us.

JOSH   Not with us?

SAM   Benny never is with us.

JOSH   Where is he then?

SAM   Lost!   Bet your life he's lost.   Come on, Josh.   If we're going let's go.

AMOS   We can't go without him.   We can't just leave him behind.

SAM   Why not?

JOSH   Benny!   Benny!

AMOS   Benny, where are you?   Benny!

BENNY   *(Off, calling distantly)* Amos!   ...   Amos!

AMOS   That's him.

BENNY   *(Off)* Sam! Sam!

SAM   He names my name upon his lips! Come on, Benny.

BENNY   *(Off)* Where are you?

AMOS   Over here, Benny, over here.

Enter Benny

AMOS   Where've you been, Benny?

BENNY   You were going too fast. I got lost.

JOSH   You can't get lost just going down to Bethlehem.

AMOS   You know the way to Bethlehem, Benny

BENNY   I know, Amos, but it's dark, and I was all confused.

SAM   So that makes a change, eh?

BENNY   All those voices, Amos ...

JOSH   Yes, we all heard the voices.

BENNY   ... I got sort of singing - in the ears - confused me.

AMOS   The angels singing, Benny.

JOSH   You saw the angels, Benny.

BENNY   No, Josh.

SAM   We all saw the angels, Benny, and the sky ablaze with light.

BENNY   I was frightened, Sam

JOSH   We were all frightened, at first ...

SAM   Not what you'd call frightened, Josh, more - startled.

JOSH   ... a bit frightened until the angel said, "Don't be afraid, I'm bringing good news."

BENNY   I didn't hear, not properly.   I covered my head.

AMOS   You didn't hear what he said?

BENNY   No, Amos.

AMOS   "I bring you good news," he said, "of great joy which will come to all the people."

JOSH   "For unto you, is born this day, in the City of David ..."

AMOS   That's Bethlehem.

JOSH   "... a Saviour who is Christ the Lord."

BENNY   Christ the Lord!

JOSH   That's what he said

BENNY   Christ the lord!

AMOS   You know who that is, Benny?   The Messiah.   The one who will set our country free.

JOSH   That's right, Amos, but best not say too much about that - not yet - might get us into trouble.

AMOS   And we're to go and find the baby lying in a manger.

JOSH   I don't know!   You must have heard the voices, Benny.

AMOS   All the angels singing "Glory to God in the highest, and on earth peace among men with whom he is pleased."

SAM   And he's not going to be very pleased with you, Benny, for not listening.

BENNY   I couldn't help it, Sam.

AMOS   Of course you couldn't, Benny.   Angels understand.

JOSH   Come on then, we must hurry.   We've got to find this stable with a baby in the manger.

SAM   And mind you stick with us, Benny.

BENNY   All right, all right.

They move on a little way

AMOS   Wait a minute, Josh.

JOSH   What's the matter now, Amos?

AMOS   Don't you realise?

JOSH   Don't I realise what?

AMOS   We're going to see a new-born baby, and a pretty important one too ...

JOSH   So what?

AMOS   ... and we haven't got any presents to give him.

SAM   Presents! How can we give him presents? It's after midnight, we've just come off the hillside. There's no time to get presents.

AMOS   There ought to be time ... time to get him presents.

JOSH   But Amos, there isn't time. We've got to go straight on.

AMOS   He didn't say so, Josh.

JOSH   He didn't say so, not in so many words, but that's what he meant.

SAM   If he meant it, why didn't he say it?

JOSH   Of course he meant it. It was clear enough to me that we were to go right away, so let's be off.

SAM   All right, Mr. Know-all. In tune with angels, is he!

JOSH   No call to be sarcastic, Sam.

AMOS   We ought to give him something.

JOSH   Oh, don't start that again, Amos.

9

BENNY   We could give him a sheep.

SAM   A sheep! Don't be daft.

BENNY   It's not daft.

SAM   What would he do with a sheep?

BENNY   He could feed it.

SAM   He can't feed himself yet. A sheep!

BENNY   Well, a lamb then.

SAM   Oh yes, you can see him, can't you, getting out of his crib and
            saying "I'm just going to feed my lamb, Mother.

JOSH   Oh shut up you two. Let's get going.

AMOS   Just a minute, Josh, babies have toys, don't they?   Dolls, things
            like that.

JOSH   Yes, but we haven't got any dolls, not here on the hillside.

AMOS   Yes we have.

JOSH   What!

AMOS   Well, you have, Josh.

JOSH   Me?

AMOS   That carving you were doing.

JOSH   He wouldn't want that.

AMOS   Why wouldn't he?

JOSH   It's only some bit of a thing I was doing to pass the time

SAM   Let's have a look at it.

JOSH   *(Getting out a rough bit of carving)*   I   mean,   he's
            somebody special isn't he?   You don't have angels singing and

shouting about any old baby, do you? It's not good enough - not good enough for the Saviour of the world.

BENNY   What is it?

SAM   What is it! Well, it's obvious isn't it? Anybody can see what it is.

BENNY   Looks like a sort of cross to me.

AMOS   It's a man. There are his arms. That's his head, isn't it Josh?

JOSH   Supposed to be.

SAM   There you are, you see, what did I tell you? Anyone can see it's a man.

AMOS   You give him that, then, Josh.

JOSH   You think he'd like it?

SAM   Of course he'd like it.

BENNY   Looks more like a cross to me.

SAM   Can't you shut up, Benny?

BENNY   I was only saying ...

SAM   Well don't say.

BENNY   ... it looks like a cross to me.

AMOS   You have to use a bit of imagination, Benny.

SAM   And a bit of common sense too, if that's possible. A cross indeed!

JOSH   If I'm going to give him my bit of carving, you'll each have to think of something. What are you going to give him, Sam?

SAM   What am I going to give him?

BENNY   Yes, Sam, what have you got to give him?

SAM Well, I'll tell you what I'm going to give, bearing in mind, mark you, that this is a baby of some importance; no less than - what did the angel call him? - the Saviour of the World. I shall give him something valuable - and useful.

AMOS Come on Sam, we're all ears.

SAM Like a shepherd, who has to save a lot of stupid sheep that get stuck in thorn bushes, or half drowned in the river, he's going to have to save a lot of stupid people who get themselves lost or in trouble. I shall give him my crook.

JOSH Your crook!

SAM My crook.

JOSH You can't give him your crook.

SAM 'Course I can.

AMOS Bravo, Sam! That's a splendid present.

JOSH But you need your crook. How'll you manage without it?

SAM I'll - well - I'll get another.

BENNY But he hasn't got any sheep.

SAM What?

BENNY The baby hasn't got any sheep.

AMOS No, Benny, of course he hasn't. But when he grows up perhaps he will.

BENNY Yes. Perhaps he'll have a great flock of 'em. He'll be glad of the crook, then.

SAM Now then, Amos, it's your turn. What precious gift do you have for him?

AMOS Not much, I'm afraid. *(producing a large pebble)* Only this.

During this conversation, Benny wanders off

SAM   A stone!

JOSH   A pebble!

AMOS   A pebble, yes, from the river.

JOSH   What do you carry that about with you for?

SAM   Not much of a present is it?

AMOS   No, not much. A dull looking thing, isn't it? ...

SAM   You're telling me!

AMOS   ... but when you dip it into water and bring it out again, it's all beautiful colours.   It's like as if all those lovely colours are locked up inside it until you dip it in the water, and all the shining wonder of it is set free for everybody too see.

JOSH   Fancy that now. Funny thing that.

SAM   You reckon he'll make sense of it?

AMOS   I reckon he will. I reckon one day he'll know more about stones and water than we ever shall.

JOSH.   Maybe. Benny's turn now, and let's hurry. We're wasting a lot of time. Where is he? Benny!

SAM   He's gone.

JOSH   Of course he's gone. I can see he's gone.

AMOS   Where's he gone. Benny! Benny, where are you?

Enter Benny carrying a wild rose

SAM   We thought we'd lost you again. Where've you been?

BENNY   I hadn't got anything, see.

SAM   Well that's no reason to go wandering off picking wild flowers without so much as a by-your-leave.

BENNY   I only picked one.

SAM   One or a dozen, what's the odds!

JOSH   We've got to be on our way, Benny, can't spend time looking for you again.

BENNY   I had to take something - for the baby.

AMOS   And you've picked a wild rose, Benny.   Well, that's nice.   It's pretty.

SAM   It will be, yes, in the daylight, but not what you'd call the ideal present to put into the tender hands of a tiny baby.

BENNY   Why not?

SAM   Why not!   You ask me why not!   I'll tell you why not, Benny my lad, it's got nasty, horrid thorns.

BENNY   Thorns ... oh.

SAM   You didn't think, did you, Benny?

BENNY   No.

SAM   You have to use a bit of common sense, see, like us.

BENNY   Oh!

SAM   There's Josh with his carving of a man - well, one day this baby will be a man himself - a proper man.

BENNY   A man - with his arms stretched out - like a cross.

AMOS   That's it, arms stretched out - calling everyone to him.

SAM   And there's me with the shepherd's crook.   A useful tool.

BENNY   Useful if he was going to be a shepherd.

SAM   I don't think he'll be a shepherd, not the Saviour of the World.

BENNY   What's wrong with being a shepherd?

SAM   Nothing wrong with it. I'm just saying. And then there's Amos with his stone ...

AMOS   Pebble.

SAM   All right, his pebble that's dull - like you, Benny -until he puts it in the water and it comes out all shining and bright - not like you, Benny.

AMOS   Who knows? One day it might happen to Benny ... might happen to any of us.

JOSH   What, dipped in the water and coming up shining?

AMOS   Just a thought.

SAM   And now, clever Benny wants to offer this baby a fistful of thorns!

BENNY   You don't think he'd like it?

SAM   I think he'd hate it.

BENNY   I never thought about the thorns.

AMOS   Of course you didn't, Benny. I mean, our hands are hard, they've got thick skin, we don't notice thorns.

SAM   And Benny's got a thick head as well. You have to think, Benny, think about the thorns.

JOSH   That's enough of that, Sam.

BENNY   P'raps I don't want to think about thorns.

JOSH   Sometimes we have to think about the thorns.

BENNY   I've got to give him something.

AMOS   It's all right, Benny. You give him the rose. I reckon that's the best gift of all.

BENNY   Really, Amos? You think so?

AMOS   'Course I do. So it's got a few thorns, but look at that lovely crown of petals.　That's what you're giving him, Benny　-　a beautiful crown.

BENNY　　Yes, a crown.　That'd make him a king, wouldn't it Amos?

AMOS　　That's right, Benny, a king.

JOSH　　All right, all right.　Let's go.　We've wasted enough time.　It'll soon be the dawn.　Come on now.

Amos and Sam follow Josh out, but Benny remains

BENNY　　A king.　That's it - a king.　The saviour of the world, he'd have to be a king.

AMOS　　*(Off)* Come on Benny.

BENNY　　*(Still rapt in his own thoughts)* Yes ... a king.

Benny leaves as the lights fade

THE END

NIMBUS PRESS PUBLICATIONS

All these Christian titles can be obtained from Moorleys Print & Publishing. A catalogue is available.
(Tel./Fax 0115 932 0643, or write to Moorleys at 23 Park Road, Ilkeston , DE7 5DA)

THE FUTURE OF THE CHURCH

MELTDOWN?   **Noel Sharp & Clifford Sharp** "Meltdown ..... pinpoints possible ways forward" REVD. ROB FROST The problem of church decline and some suggestions for thought and action from a Methodist minister and a Local Preacher. ISBN 1 874424 66 7

SKETCHES

CELEBRATING LIGHT Sketches for churches on the theme of 'light' to celebrate the Christian women's group, Network's 10th anniversary. Includes a prizewinner from the Nimbus Press Christian Playwriting Competition 1997. ISBN 1 874424

SKETCHES FOR SEEKER SERVICES: 1 11 sketches originally used in worship and evangelistic services presenting the Christian faith in a way that non-Christians can understand. Christian approaches to crime & punishment, money, God & science, unemployment etc. and modern parables. ISBN 1 874424 71 3

SKETCHES FOR SEEKER SERVICES: 2 Volume 2. University Challenge with a 'big' question, a Christian wins the lottery, false pictures of Christians, forgiveness, recipe for Christian living etc. ISBN 1 874424 81 0

IS THIS YOUR LIFE? & PEARL OF GREAT PRICE   **Clifford Sharp**   A 12min. spoof of the TV programme. Used with teenagers. And a short play for children, used in a Junior Church anniversary (Narrator, small speaking parts,10mins). ISBN 1 874424 76 4

BIBLICAL - JESUS AND FAMILY, DISCIPLES

TIME TO SPEAK   **Ronald Rich**   Prizewinner in the Nimbus Press Christian Playwriting Competition 1997. A play about an encounter between Peter and Pilate in Rome in AD 64. Based on historical possibility - Pilate's Christian wife is causing him practical problems and some soul-searching about his past. (5m 2f. 30mins) ISBN 1 874424 96 9

THE PRICE OF OLIVES   **Clifford Sharp**   "I am delighted that this play explores ... the Hidden years of the youth of Jesus. The joys and strains of family life are well depicted, in a community that was human as well as holy and serves as a model for our times." - PROFESSOR GEOFFREY PARRINDER. (5m 2f,40mins)   ISBN 1 874424 46 2

CHRISTMAS

ANGEL'S COUNSEL   **Rosi MorganBarry**   Winner of the Nimbus Press Christian Playwriting Competition 1997. The Christmas Nativity is cleverly and seamlessly woven into the story of a fairytale King and Queen. For primary schools, Junior Church, theatre groups playing to children, or adults. (10 speaking parts, some non-speaking, 30 mins)   ISBN 1 874424 86 1

LOOKING FOR A KING Jonathan Curnow (2m 2f,20mins and 2m 1f,20mins) The title play "illustrates 1st century Jewish hopes for a warrior Messiah to rid the land of Romans ... Down to Earth depicts a young man determined to spend a month in prison, though he has committed no crime ... there are strong echoes of the Christmas story of God the Father sending His Son into the world." REVD. MICHAEL SKINNER, FORMER PRINCIPAL WESLEY HOUSE, CAMBRIDGE.   ISBN 1 874424 31 4

LETS GO TO BETHLEHEM   **Edward Bennett**   With funny and touching dialogue 4 shepherds make their way to Bethlehem wondering what they can give the baby Jesus. The first performance was by adults but it is also "suitable for older children bored with traditional nativity plays" RADIUS - The Religious Drama Assoc. of Britain. (4m,15mins) ISBN 1 874424 36 5

DRAMA FOR ADULTS OR CHILDREN

LETS GO TO BETHLEHEM, IS THIS YOUR LIFE? & PEARL OF GREAT PRICE (above)

THE GOLDEN AGE   **Clifford Sharp**   How might the twentieth century look to people living in 2192? 'The Golden Age' deals in a light-hearted way with serious environmental issues. The scene is an imaginary broadcast so that, if desired, all parts may be read from a script. Simple staging incorporates music and recorded voices. Suitable for schools. (2m 1f 3 either,30mins)   ISBN 1 874424 10 1

THE SEARCH FOR THE TRUE CHURCH

MY KIND OF GOD   **Clifford Sharp**   In the title play 'respectable' meets 'outcast'. It was first performed at the Methodist Conference. "written by a prison visitor which made it all the more poignant ..." THE METHODIST RECORDER. New Churches for Old has an ecumenical theme - different churches compete for a new recruit. (2m 1f,12mins and 3m 3f,8mins) ISBN 1 874424 41 1

THE GOOD CHURCH GUIDE   **Jonathan Curnow**   At a meeting chaired by the mysterious Elisabeth, representatives of five churches in 'Lessingham' each argue that theirs is the true one that should be included in the new "Good Church Guide". Which will be chosen - the 'Bible-based' Free Evangelicals, St Stephens with its musical excellence, Blackmill United with its relevant social gospel, the Anglo-Catholics of St Botolphs, or the 'real' Catholics of the Immaculate Conception? (4m 3f,15mins) ISBN 1 874424 51 9

EASTER

THE ROSE HAS THORNS   **Edward Bennett**   A nurse visits the Holy Land and 2 years later, working in a war zone, reflects again upon the passion of Christ as she learns the cost of love and sacrifice, but also the possibility of hope in the midst of suffering. (3f 3m,25mins)   ISBN 1 874424 56 X